SCIENCE FILES
ELECTRICITY & MAGNETISM

SCIENCE FILES – ELECTRICITY AND MAGNETISM
was produced by

David West 웃웃 Children's Books

7 Princeton Court
55 Felsham Road
London SW15 1AZ

Designer: Rob Shone
Editor: Gail Bushnell
Picture Research: Carlotta Cooper

First published in Great Britain by Heinemann
Library, Halley Court, Jordan Hill, Oxford
OX2 8EJ, part of Harcourt Education.
Heinemann is a registered trademark
of Harcourt Education Ltd.

08 07 06 05
10 9 8 7 6 5 4 3 2 1

ISBN 0 431 14318 8 (HB)
ISBN 0 431 14325 0 (PB)

British Library Cataloguing in Publication Data

Parker, Steve
Electricity & magnetism. - (Science files)
1. Electricity - Juvenile literature 2. Magnetism -
Juvenile literature 3. Electricity - Experiments -
Juvenile literature 4. Magnetism- Experiments -
Juvenile literature
I. Title
537

Printed and bound in China

PHOTO CREDITS :
Abbreviations: t-top, m-middle, b-bottom, r-right,
l-left, c-centre.

Front cover - tl & bm - Corbis Images, bl -
National Oceanic & Atmospheric Administration
(NOAA). Pages 3 & 6t, 4–5 & 10 - National
Oceanic & Atmospheric Administration (NOAA).
7r, 8, 10–11, 11r, 15l, 16, 17t & m, 18, 18–19,
19l, 20t, 22r, 22–23, 23, 24l, 28, 28–29, 29t -
Corbis Images. 8–9, 12, 14b - Rex Features Ltd.
12–13 (Speaker System 004), 21b (0B250037):
budgetstockphoto.com. 13l - BSky B.

Every effort has been made to contact copyright
holders of any material reproduced in this book.
Any omissions will be rectified in subsequent
printings if notice is given to the publishers.

With special thanks to the models: Felix Blom,
Tucker Bryant and Margaux Monfared.

*An explanation of difficult words can be
found in the glossary on page 31.*

SCIENCE FILES

ELECTRICITY & MAGNETISM

Steve Parker

Heinemann
LIBRARY

CONTENTS

WARNING!
All projects should be supervised by a responsible adult. Some need extra care and expert help, and are marked with a red box. Make sure the instructions are followed. *Never take risks.*

INTRODUCTION

What do a light bulb, a note-holding fridge-magnet, a medical scanner which looks inside the body, and a vacuum-cleaner have in common? They all work by electricity, or magnetism, or both – using one of the most basic forces in the whole Universe. Without them, modern life would come to a cold dark halt.

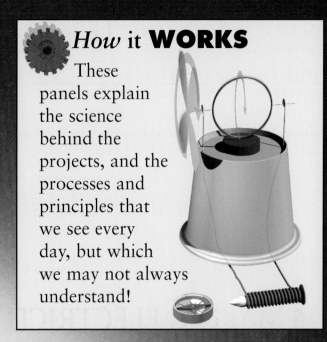

How it **WORKS**

These panels explain the science behind the projects, and the processes and principles that we see every day, but which we may not always understand!

PROJECTS

The projects are simple to do with supervision, using household items. Remember – scientists are cautious. They prepare equipment thoroughly, they know what should happen, and they *always* put safety first.

Static electricity (electrostatic charge) builds up in clouds until powerful enough to leap to the ground as a flash of lightning.

Electricity creates giant lightning bolts and powers huge machines, but it is based on some of the tiniest particles of all – electrons.

ALL THINGS ARE ATOMS

Everything in the Universe, from a speck of dust to massive stars deep in space, is made of minute pieces called atoms. They are so small, this full stop contains millions of them.

COLLECT STATIC

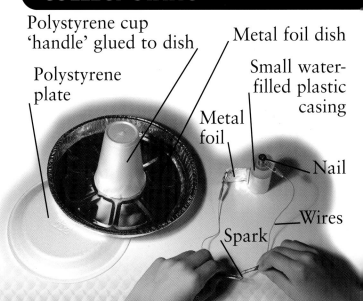

Polystyrene cup 'handle' glued to dish

Metal foil dish

Polystyrene plate

Small water-filled plastic casing

Metal foil

Nail

Wires

Spark

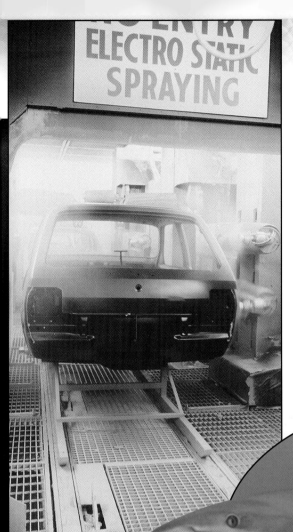

Substances with opposite static charges attract. If the car is positive and paint negative, the paint sticks better.

ELECTRONS ON THE GO = ELECTRICITY

Inside an atom, particles called protons and neutrons clump in a central nucleus, and around this whizz yet more particles – electrons. Rubbing a substance can cause electrons to detach from their atoms, ready to 'jump' to other atoms. This is static electricity or electric charge. Billions of electrons all 'hopping' steadily from atom to atom, in the same direction, form the flow of energy we call electric current.

Animal muscles give out tiny electrical pulses which pass through water. A shark can detect them to find its prey.

A capacitor stores static or electric charge. Make one as shown left.

Rub wool on the polystyrene plate for a minute, then touch it to the dish. Hold the dish by its 'handle' and touch it briefly to the foil and nail. Bring the wires connecting them together. Watch for a spark.

WARNING Charging the capacitor more than four times can store enough static electricity to give a small shock if you touch the foil and nail. Handle with care.

How it WORKS

Rubbing the plate makes electrons come away from their atoms, forming static charge. The charge passes to the metal foil dish when touched, and then to the nail and water in the plastic casing. When wires link the foil and nail, the charge evens out with a tiny spark.

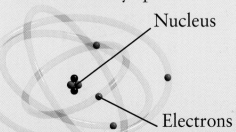

Nucleus

Electrons

Spark

Positive charge

Negative charge

ABOUT MAGNETISM

Magnetism is most mysterious. This invisible force affects only certain substances, and like electricity, it comes from the tiniest parts of atoms – electrons.

IN A SPIN

Electricity is due to the movement of 'free' electrons jumping from atom to atom. Magnetism is due to the way electrons spin around like tiny tops, as they swirl about inside their atoms. If the spinning directions of all the electrons in billions of atoms line up in a certain way, the result is a magnetic force which can push, pull, twist and turn.

This magnetic resonance imaging scanner uses a powerful magnetic field. The resulting MRI scan gives the doctor a picture of the patient's insides.

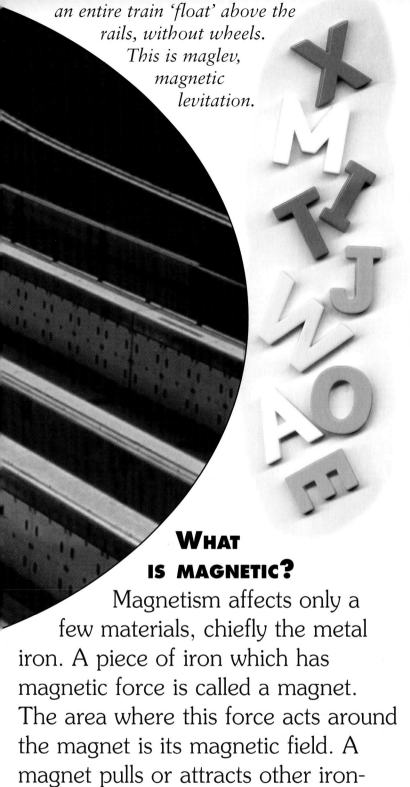

Magnetism is strong enough to make an entire train 'float' above the rails, without wheels. This is maglev, magnetic levitation.

Magnets can hold letters on metal surfaces, such as fridges (left). Each letter has a disc magnet, which has a pole on each side.

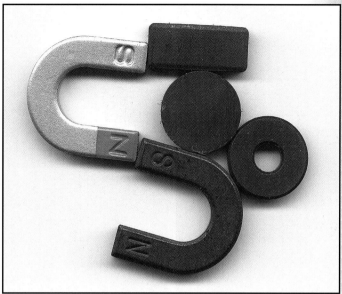

Different shapes do different jobs. Ring magnets have poles on the inner and outer rings. Horseshoes have a pole at each end.

WHAT IS MAGNETIC?

Magnetism affects only a few materials, chiefly the metal iron. A piece of iron which has magnetic force is called a magnet. The area where this force acts around the magnet is its magnetic field. A magnet pulls or attracts other iron-containing objects, which are said to be magnetic. Steel is a mix of various substances, mainly iron, so steel is magnetic too.

How it WORKS

A magnet's field is strongest in two places called poles. These have opposing forces to each other, called North (N or +), and South (S or -). With two magnets, poles of the same kind push apart, or repel. Poles of opposite kinds pull together, or attract.

Opposite poles attract

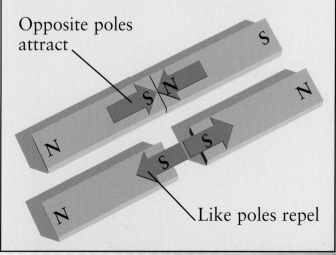

Like poles repel

9

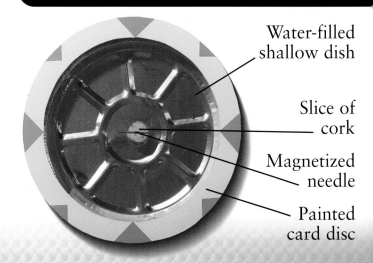

We cannot see magnetic force, which is just as well, because it is all around us. The Earth is a giant magnet, whose magnetism has long been used by people.

THE SPINNING CORE

Deep inside the Earth is the planet's core, a vast ball of red-hot, iron-rich rocks. The rock is heated so much, it can flow like treacle. As the Earth spins around daily, the core swirls around too, and makes magnetism.

The Sun's 'solar wind' consists of billions of tiny electrically charged particles. They hit Earth's magnetism high above and glow as auroras (northern and southern lights).

POINTING TO THE POLES

Water-filled shallow dish

Slice of cork

Magnetized needle

Painted card disc

FINDING THE WAY

A compass is a long, slim magnet, often shaped like a needle, which can turn or swivel easily. Due to attraction and repulsion, its own poles swing around to line up with the Earth's magnetic force, and point to the magnetic North and South Poles.

Migrating whales, fish, and birds like these stilts may find their way using Earth's magnetic field.

VERY USEFUL

People have used compasses to navigate across land and sea for a thousand years. Some animals have a 'natural compass' in their bodies to find their way on migration.

A magnetic compass is used to position the map correctly as people travel through the wilderness.

A steel needle stroked the same way 20-plus times, with the same end of a magnet, becomes a magnet itself.

Put it on to a slice of floating cork. It always points the same way.

How it WORKS

The magnetized needle works like a compass, being affected by the magnetic field surrounding Earth. The field is made of invisible lines of magnetic force. One end of the compass is attracted to the planet's North Pole and the other to the South Pole.

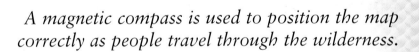

Magnetic North Pole

Earth's lines of magnetic force

Compasses align with magnetic field

Magnetic South Pole

Massive electromagnets in ironworks, steel factories and scrap yards can lift magnetic objects weighing many tonnes. Non-magnetic (non-iron) materials are left behind – a useful way of sorting scrap metals for recycling.

Wherever there is electricity, there's also magnetism. An electric current flowing through a wire makes a magnetic field around the wire. This is the electromagnetic effect.

A loudspeaker has both kinds of magnets. Electric signals in the electromagnet make it push and pull against the magnet, moving the speaker cone.

ON AND OFF

If the current-carrying wire is looped into a coil around an iron rod or bar, called the core, this makes its magnetism much stronger. The resulting device is known as an electromagnet. The magnetism of an electromagnet is the same as the magnetism from a magnet, except for one feature. If an electromagnet's current is turned off, its magnetism disappears.

MAKE AN ELECTROMAGNET

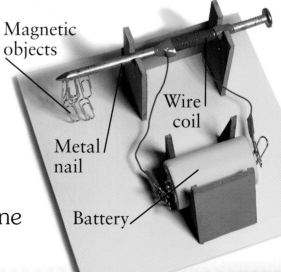

Magnetic objects

Metal nail

Wire coil

Battery

PULLING POWER

A solenoid is similar to an electromagnet. It has a moveable iron core at one end of the coil. Switching on makes the core slide quickly into the centre of the coil. Turning off allows a spring to pull it back again.

Wires buried in floors and roads have magnetic fields around them. These can be detected and followed by robot transporters in factories.

EVERYDAY HELPERS

We use electromagnets and solenoids many times daily, without realizing. They are found in loudspeakers, 'ding-dong' doorbells and the sliding bolts in remote-control security locks on cars and house doors.

Electromagnets in 'tube'-type televisions move the beam of electrons that builds up the picture on screen.

A large iron nail and plastic-coated wire make a simple electromagnet.

Wind the wire tightly at least 20 times round the nail – more turns make stronger magnetism. Connect the wire's ends to a battery – more volts make more magnetism – so try a 9 volt battery. The electromagnet will attract magnetic objects.

How it WORKS

Most iron-based substances have tiny areas of magnetism called domains. Normally these are all mixed up, pointing in different directions, so they cancel out. A nearby electric current makes the domains point in the same direction, so their magnetism adds up to make a strong magnetic field.

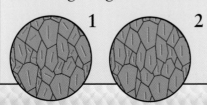

1   **2**

S — Circuit of electricity

N — Nail becomes magnet with poles

Electricity changes the tiny domains from random (**1**) to aligned (**2**).

Electricity produces magnetism, in an electromagnet – and the opposite is true. Magnetism can make electricity. This effect also occurs many times in daily life.

MOVING OR CHANGING

When a wire and magnet move in relation to each other, electricity flows in the wire. This is known as electromagnetic (EM) induction. It does not matter if the wire stays still and the magnetic field around it moves, or the field is still and the wire moves – electric current is still induced.

In some trains, diesel engines drive generators that make electricity for motors. Both the generators and motors work using electromagnetic induction.

A metal-detector makes a magnetic field around itself. An iron-based object distorts the field, triggering the sensor.

MAKE A WIND TURBINE

Electromagnet is switched on by current

Link wires

Coil

Wire holder

Windmill

Magnet

Compass moves when current flows

Make a small electric current using wind.

Push paperclip wire holders into a paper cup and position magnet. Make a wire coil. Scrape the insulation off one side of each end of the coil wire (see close-up on page 25). Thread the ends through the holders. Fix a windmill to one end. Connect link wires to the holders (inside cup) and then to the electromagnet (see page 12).

Wind turbines are another form of generator. However, they use natural power as an energy source.

CHANGING STRENGTH

Even if the magnetic field and the wire stay still, electricity can still be induced. This happens if the field changes in strength, becoming more or less powerful.

INDUCTION EVERYWHERE

EM induction is used in all kinds of devices, from electric guitars to traffic lights. With its 'opposite', the electromagnetic effect, it is essential in machines such as generators and motors, as shown later.

How it WORKS

When the wind blows, the compass moves! As the coil turns near the magnet, an induced current flows around the coil. It flows down one wire holder and link wire to the electromagnet, and then back to the coil. The electromagnet's field attracts the magnetic compass. A rule describes this movement.

RIGHT-HAND RULE

Movement of coil (thumb)

Direction of magnetic field (first finger)

Direction of current (second finger)

The 'right-hand rule' shows the current's direction according to the magnetic field and coil motion.

A guitar's strings move in the magnetism of the pick-up, creating electricity in the pick-up's wire coil.

Pick-up with wire coil around

Electrical energy is so useful because it can be made from many other kinds of energy – and changed back into them, too.

A control room engineer checks the amount of electricity being produced in a power station.

SOURCES OF ELECTRICITY

Many energy forms can be converted directly into electric current, including chemicals, heat, movement and light. There are chemicals inside batteries and the fuels burned in power stations, heat and movement can be found in power station generators and light for solar panels and small solar cells is used in calculators.

How it **WORKS**

There are many designs of battery, but a typical version has two metallic electrodes – anode (+) and cathode (-). There is a paste or powder electrolyte between them. Chemical changes between electrodes and electrolyte make electrons leave their atoms, flow out from the negative contact along a wire, back to the positive.

ALTERNATE OR DIRECT?

The way power station generators work means their electricity flows one way, then the other, and so on – reversing itself 50 or 60 times each second. This type of flow is known as alternating current, AC. Batteries (electrical cells) make a steady one-way flow of electricity called direct current, DC.

Solar panels have thousands of button-sized photovoltaic cells. The Sun's light energy knocks electrons from their atoms to make the electric current.

Water piled up behind a hydro-electric dam flows along pipes to fan-like turbines in huge casings, which turn electricity generators.

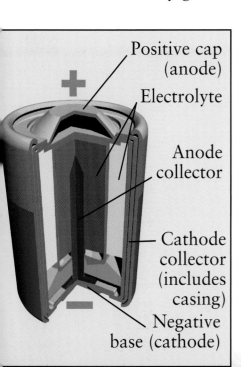

Positive cap (anode)

Electrolyte

Anode collector

Cathode collector (includes casing)

Negative base (cathode)

INSIDE A BATTERY

Batteries are convenient 'parcels' of chemicals which react together to make electrons come away from their atoms. This only happens when the battery is linked by wires to an electrical device, and the electrons have somewhere to flow. Otherwise there is no reaction.

A rechargeable battery uses the electricity put in to reverse the chemical reactions, so it can give out electricity again.

17

Electricity does not flow unless it has somewhere to go. Usually this is around a continuous pathway from its source, out and back again.

CIRCUITS

Electricity's pathway is known as a circuit. Parts of the circuit are metal wires, which carry electricity well. The circuit can also include useful components, such as a small light bulb or a huge electric motor. The current flowing through these components makes them work.

Railway power lines carry current many kilometres, with the train motors as part of the very long circuit.

MAKE A CIRCUIT BOARD

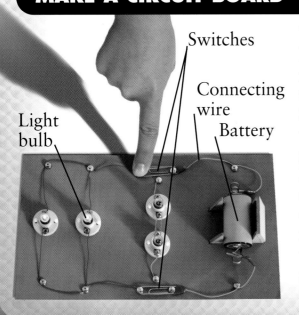

Switches

Connecting wire

Battery

Light bulb

You can make a circuit board with several paths for a battery's electricity, through wires and bulbs. Switches can be made with paperclips between gaps in the wire circuit. By using the switches to connect to different parts of the circuit you can make either the bulbs on the left, or those on the right, light up. Which ones are the brightest?

How it WORKS

In a series circuit (1), electricity flows through each component in turn. Its 'push' in volts is shared and so the bulbs glow dimmer. In a parallel circuit (2), current flows at full power through all components, and so the bulbs glow brighter.

In some circuits, wires are replaced by metal strips on a sheet-like board. These circuit boards are found in many electrical appliances, such as televisions and computers.

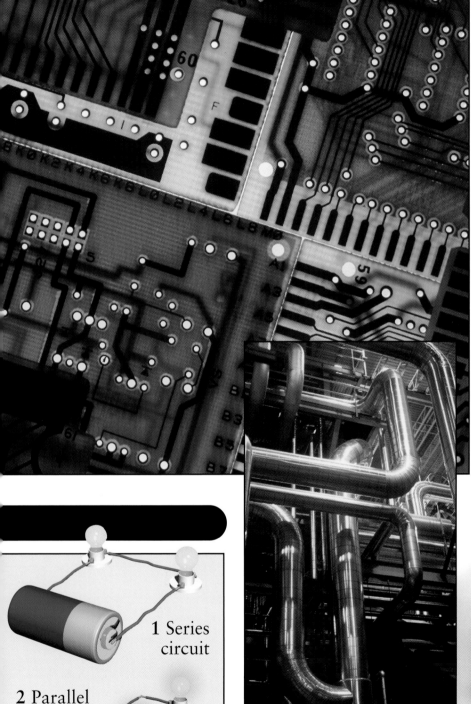

1 Series circuit

2 Parallel circuit

Wires carrying huge amounts of electricity in factories are usually protected from damage by tubes known as conduits.

ON AND OFF

Most circuits contain a component known as a switch. When this is 'on' it makes a path for electricity and allows it to flow around the complete circuit. Turn it 'off' and it makes a small break or gap. Electricity cannot pass through the air in the gap and so it stops.

MANY PATHWAYS

Simple circuits, like those in torches and toys, have just one pathway for electricity. Others have hundreds of wires and other connectors and thousands of components. The current is shared between the components depending on how they are joined.

A car's spark plug has a tiny gap at the bottom. However the electricity is powerful enough (in volts) to leap across this as a spark.

Electricity travels huge distances to our homes, schools, offices and factories. Making it and distributing it are massive industries.

Power stations run day and night to keep up supplies.

VOLTAGE

Electricity is measured in various ways. Its force or pushing strength is measured in volts. A torch-type battery produces just a few volts. Car batteries are usually 12 or 24 volts. The mains electricity from wall sockets is 240 volts – which is strong enough to kill. In big overhead power lines the electricity may be 400,000 volts or more – enough to supply thousands of homes.

Electricity enters a building through a consumer unit. This has circuit-breakers to switch off the current if there is a fault.

MAKE A DIMMER SWITCH

Use a coil of bare copper wire wound on a card tube and connected to a battery to make a dimmer switch.

The battery's other terminal leads to a bulb and then a bare-ended wire – the wiper. Move the wiper along the coil and watch the bulb.

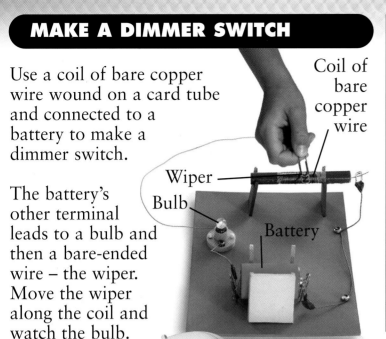

Coil of bare copper wire

Wiper

Bulb

Battery

How it **WORKS**

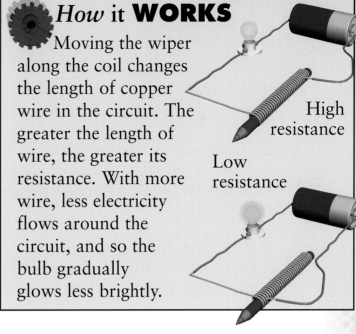

Moving the wiper along the coil changes the length of copper wire in the circuit. The greater the length of wire, the greater its resistance. With more wire, less electricity flows around the circuit, and so the bulb gradually glows less brightly.

High resistance

Low resistance

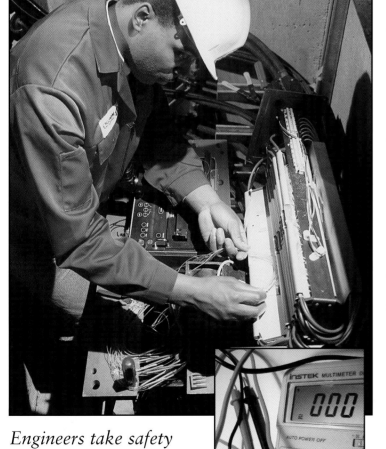

Engineers take safety precautions when they check problems. A fault may mean that a wire which should only have a few volts has more.

RESIST THE FLOW

Amps (ampères) show the quantity or amount of current. One amp is over six billion billion electrons per second! Ohms measure resistance – how easily a substance or object carries electric current. As the resistance goes up, the electricity passing through goes down.

WHAT'S A WATT?

The rate at which energy is used or changed is known in science as power, and is measured in watts. Electricity is energy, and so its use is counted in watts. In an electrical circuit, the number of watts equals the volts multiplied by the amps.

The multimeter is adjusted to measure volts (V), amps (A), ohms (Ω) or other units.

We usually join electrical parts like bulbs and batteries with wires. Why? Because the metal of a wire carries electricity well – it is a good conductor.

EASY FLOW

Nearly all metals are good conductors. One of the best is silver. Yet it is too costly for general use, apart from special equipment such as certain computer parts. One of the next best is copper, which is cheaper, and is used for wires in homes and buildings.

A lightning conductor is a metal strap which runs from the top of a tall building, such as the Eiffel Tower. It carries the surge of lightning safely into the ground.

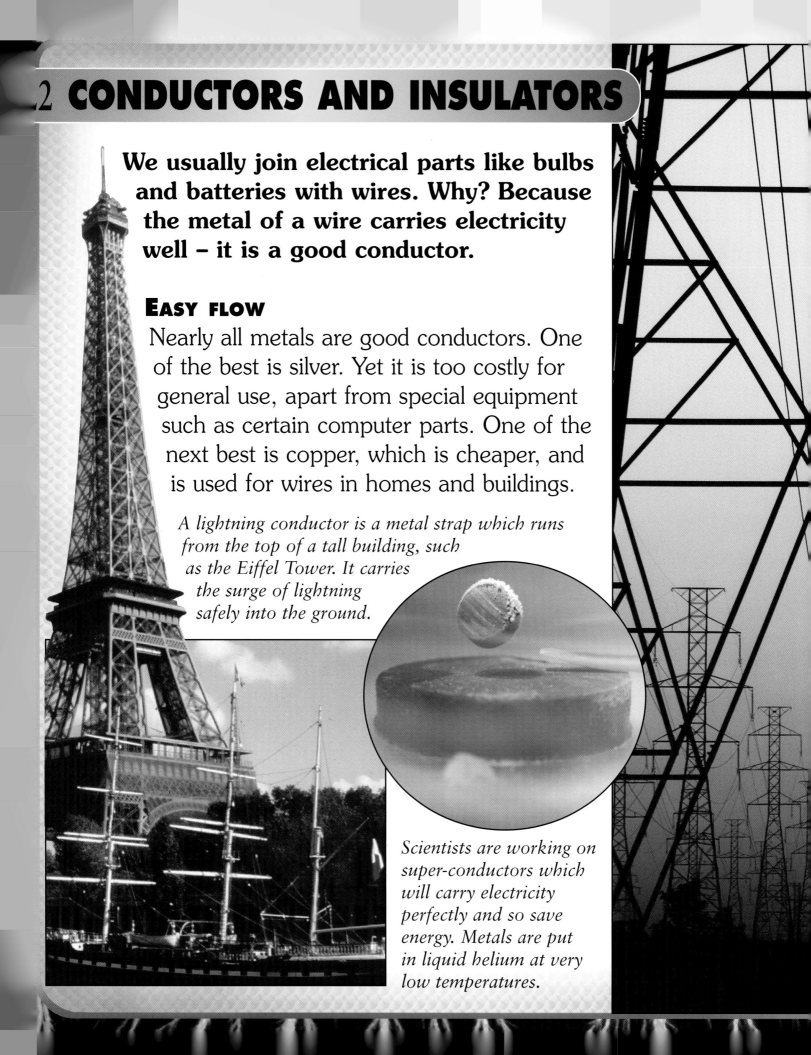

Scientists are working on super-conductors which will carry electricity perfectly and so save energy. Metals are put in liquid helium at very low temperatures.

Massive copper wires would be heavy and unsuitable for overhead power lines. So other metals are used, including lightweight aluminium.

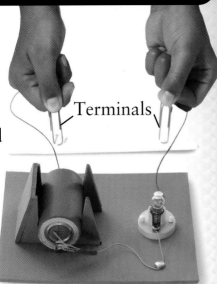

NO FLOW

An insulator is a substance that has a very high resistance – it is very bad at carrying electricity. Examples include wood, glass, paper, card, rubber, plastics, and ceramics such as pottery. Semiconductors carry some electricity or not, depending on how they are used.

Materials to be tested

Terminals

Use a simple circuit to test if materials are conductors.

Touch the paperclip terminals to substances, like foil, wood plastic, and the 'lead' of a pencil. Does the bulb light?

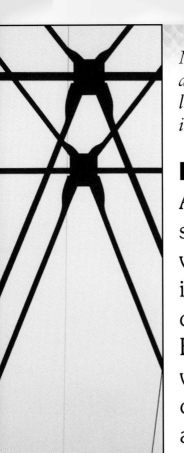

High-voltage wires at a power station have disc-like insulators to prevent current leaking into the ground.

How it **WORKS**

The test substance completes the electrical circuit through the bulb. If the substance is a good conductor, the maximum electricity flows and the bulb glows brightly. If it is an effective insulator, hardly any current passes and the bulb stays unlit. Semi-conductors cause a faint glow. Card is usually a good insulator, but try card soaked in water. Does the result mean that water is a conductor?

23

Great lengths of electrical wiring have been wound on to drums, by using motors to turn the drums. The wires will be wrapped into coils – for more electric motors.

One of the most useful of all machines is the motor. It changes electrical energy into the spinning movement that drives countless machines and gadgets.

ATTRACT AND REPEL

Most motors use the electromagnetic effect. Current flows through a wire coil on an axle or shaft. The coil becomes an electromagnet. Nearby is another magnet. The two magnetic fields interact, alternately attracting and repelling to make the coil spin on its shaft.

City-street and subway trains use electric motors. They speed up and slow down quickly and release no harmful fumes unlike petrol or diesel engines.

IN A SPIN

See how a motor works by adapting the wind-turbine (page 15).

Scrape the insulation off one side of each end of the coil wire. Connect the battery to the wire holders with the coil resting between the holders. If the coil does not start to spin, give it a little push. When electrical current flows through the coil, does it move – and which way?

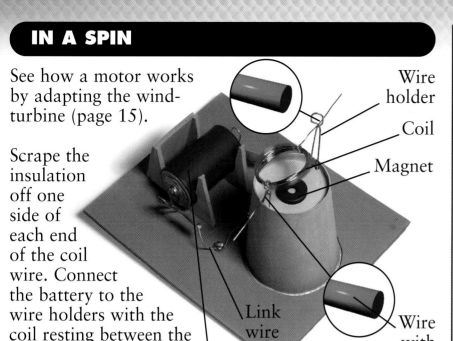

Wire holder
Coil
Magnet
Link wire
Battery
Wire with insulation on one side

WARNING Disconnect battery after two minutes to prevent the wire holders from getting hot.

SWITCHED AROUND

In a DC (battery) motor, for every turn of the coil, the current is reversed, and switched back again, so the magnetic fields push and pull at the correct times. A rotating switch on the shaft, the commutator, does this. Some AC motors lack a commutator since the current reverses itself.

ENERGY EFFICIENT

Motors change over two-thirds of electrical energy into motion – much more than petrol or diesel engines.

How it WORKS

Electric current passes along the link wires and through the coil, making it an electromagnet with two poles. These attract or repel the poles of the small magnet, depending on which way the current flows. Using half insulated wire makes the current switch on and off to keep the coil spinning. The coil's movement is described by a rule.

LEFT-HAND RULE

Movement of coil (thumb)

Direction of magnetic field (first finger)

Direction of current (second finger)

The 'left-hand rule' shows the motor's motion according to the magnetic field and current.

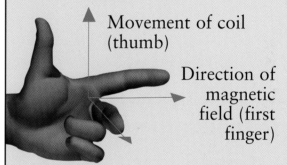

Magnets

Coils

Motors in appliances and tools have many sets of coils (above) and spin within curved magnets.

On a cold winter's night, people at home dim the lights, turn up the heating and TV, settle down to watch, then CLICK ...

OH NO!

... It's a power cut! The house goes dark, silent and cold. Only at these times do we realize how much we rely on electricity for light, heat, sound, vision, computers, internet and so on.

Massive stores are devoted to selling myriad electric gadgets, appliances and tools. Electrical energy is usually quiet, clean and efficient – but must be kept safe at all times.

Night turns into day at the flick of a switch, allowing people to work or play at any hour. In cold places, heating uses far more electricity than lighting.

COVERED WITH COPPER

Anode and cathode in the electrolyte.

WARNING An adult should supervise this project. The materials can get hot, so handle with care.

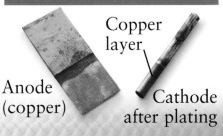

Copper layer

Anode (copper)

Cathode after plating

Electrically powered robots replace human muscle power for many factory tasks such as welding cars.

SPECIALIST USES

Many gadgets and appliances we buy are powered by electricity – and made by it too. Factories are full of electric motors, drills and other tools. One specialized method is electroplating, using electricity to cover one substance with a thin layer of another substance. Items which look valuable, as if made of 'solid' gold or silver, may be ordinary metal underneath.

Electroplating covers every tiny nook and cranny, atom by atom. It can plate a cheap dull metal with shiny chromium.

Electric cars are gradually becoming powerful and fast. A problem is the limited distance they can travel before their batteries need a recharge – which can take hours.

In electroplating, a current passes between two terminals, the positive anode and negative cathode. Try it yourself.

Use a piece of copper for the anode and steel for the cathode, with dissolved Epsom salts as the electrolyte for the current to pass through. Leave it for a day.

How it WORKS

The electricity makes atoms of copper leave the anode, when they gain a positive charge. They are then called ions. They float in the electrolyte and are drawn to the negative terminal of the cathode, where they stick tight.

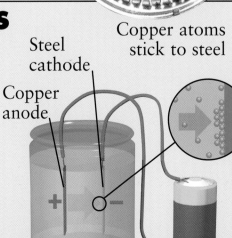

Steel cathode

Copper anode

Copper atoms stick to steel

Microchips are usually smaller than a fingernail, protected in black plastic cases, and joined into circuits by metal contacts around the edge.

Electronic devices make sounds and pictures, control and measure, calculate and memorize. But when does electric become electronic?

SMALLER

Size and movement are the key. A washing machine is electrical, with moving parts. The only moving parts in the electronic microchip, which controls it, are electrons.

Dozens of microchips fit on to a silicon wafer, smaller than a CD.

CHIPS EVERYWHERE

Electronic devices called microchips are small slices or 'chips' of a semiconductor substance, silicon. Millions of microscopic parts and components are etched or 'carved' on to the chip's surface by laser light, chemicals and other techniques.

How it WORKS

When a microchip is made, all the components are in position, already connected together or integrated. So microchips are also known as ICs, integrated circuits.

1 Silicon wafers

2 Circuits printed on wafer

3 Wafer cut into chips

4 Finished chip

The biggest computers are called mainframes. They are used for immense tasks like controlling a space mission or predicting the weather.

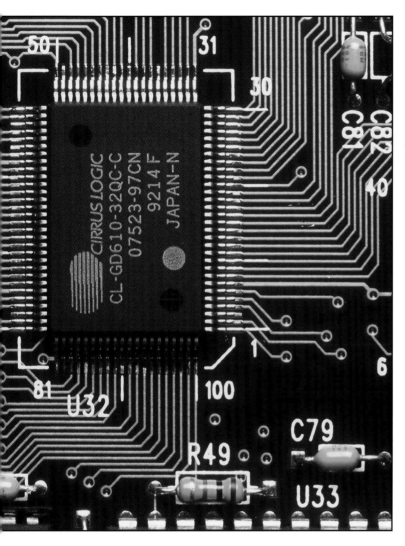

Older planes had electrical dials and switches. Modern planes have electronic touch-screens.

FASTER THAN THINKING

A chip's components form incredibly complex circuits which send and receive so many electrical signals, so fast, that they almost think like you!

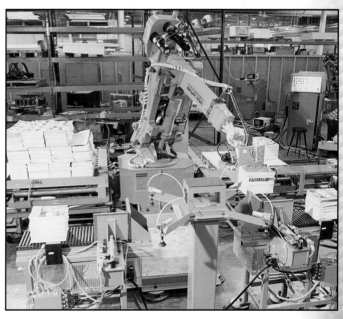

An electrical machine, like a robot, usually has an electronic microchip 'brain' which tells it what to do.

29

VOLTS, AMPS, OHMS AND WATTS

The volt measures the pushing strength of electricity. This is potential difference (pd), or electromotive force (emf) – see panel, right. The ampère (amp) measures the quantity of electrical charge flowing past, one amp being about 6.28 billion billion electrons passing per second. The ohm is the resistance or opposition to this flow. These units are linked by one of the most important laws in electrical engineering, known as Ohm's law:

$$V \text{ (volts)} = I \text{ (amps)} \times R \text{ (ohms)}$$

The watt is a unit of power, that is, the rate of using or converting energy. It applies to all energy forms, but with electricity:

$$W \text{ (watts)} = V \text{ (volts)} \times I \text{ (amps)}$$

ELECTRICAL CHARGE

Electrical charge is, or is caused by, electrons separated from their atoms and ready to flow or actually moving. It is measured in coulombs. One coulomb is the amount of charge that makes up a current of one amp (see above). Capacitors store charge and are rated in farads. One farad is a store or capacitance of one coulomb per volt.

HOW MANY VOLTS?

Major cross-country power lines	400,000 plus
Local power lines, railways	33,000
Smaller factories, workshops	440
Mains supply (UK/US)	220/110
Telephone ringing signal	50–100
Truck and tractor batteries	24
Car batteries	12
Portable 'powerpack' battery	9
Typical LED display	5
Torch battery	1.5
Nerve signal in human body	0.01

MAGNETIC UNITS

The strength of a magnetic field over the whole area of the field, which is like the total 'quantity' of magnetism, is called magnetic flux. It is measured in webers (Wb). The strength of a magnetic field in a certain area, which is like the number of lines of magnetic force in that area, is magnetic flux density. It is measured in teslas (T). One tesla is one weber per square metre.

HOW MANY WATTS?

1000 watts would power average examples of these devices for this long:

Instant-heat shower	5–10 minutes
Electric kettle	30 minutes
Microwave oven	30–60 minutes
Standard electric heater	1 hour
Food processor	2–3 hours
Home computer	3–5 hours
Large-screen television	5 hours
Standard light bulb (100W)	10 hours
Electric toothbrush	30-plus hours

STRENGTH OF MAGNETIC FIELD

Comparative strengths of magnetic fields, in teslas, include:

Most powerful fields for scientific research	40
Scrapyard magnet or medical MRI scanner	1–5
Fridge magnet	0.1
Earth's field at pole	0.00006
Earth's field at equator	0.000025
Nerve signals in brain	0.000000001

GLOSSARY

anode
An electrode connected to the positive terminal (+) of a battery or other electricity source.

atom
The smallest particle of an element, made up of a central nucleus surrounded by electrons.

cathode
An electrode connected to the negative terminal (-) of a battery or other electricity source.

conduction
When energy, such as heat or electricity, moves through an object or from one object to another.

current
In electricity, the quantity or amount of electrical energy, in terms of numbers of electrons. It is measured in amps.

domain
A tiny area of magnetism within a magnet.

electrode
A contact or terminal through which electricity passes in or out of a substance.

electromagnetic effect
When an electric current flows through a wire or similar conductor and creates a magnetic field around the wire.

electromagnetic induction
When a wire or similar conductor moves in a magnetic field, or the field changes in strength, and creates a flow of electricity.

insulate
To stop electricity by covering with a non-conducting material.

photovoltaic cell
A device that changes light energy directly into electrical energy, with no stages in between.

resistance
To oppose or act against the flow of electricity.